58792782R10057

Made in the USA
Columbia, SC
24 May 2019